Crossroads and/or Illusions

Coping with Plug & Play
Ideology

By Aleksandar Krzavac

ISBN 978-1-365-81306-1

Front Cover Photo Courtesy of goodfreephotos.com

Table of Contents

Note

This book is, let`s say, mixture of journalist style and semi-scientific reports and analyses on one side, and personal, to some extent, autobiographical impressions over ongoing world happenings on the other side. It`s impossible to make great historical wisdom on 50 pages that would solve all problems at the ease of headache pill. Some indictments against war criminals and/or serial killers have 1,000 pages, or even more.

My book is not crowded with table and graphs for I don't want to bother readers with cosmetics, making up hot issues that must be taken seriously. Graphs and tables are more kind of special visual effects for eyes, words are stuff that matter that should break into our brains. That's the only way to figure out, or at least to try to figure out what's going around us.

At this point even understanding is enough, and allowed, as first step to long journey of world continual changing to its optimal status. I do hope this work is a small piece of contribution to (re)defining some basic values and standards.

Bentleys, Bayliners & Basic needs

Issue of Basic Needs is one of crucial and most sensitive in one world that would be sooner or later be run as „global village". Each revolution, no matter whether fierce and visible or calm and in „backstage", per se, is highly disruptive and unpredictable regarding its consequences. That applies to spreading postindustrial society worldwide too. Unfortunately, at first sight, there are much more losers than winners in globalization process. Never, so far, gap between rich and poor has been so big. Even Ancient Egypt pharaohs would have been driven mad by wealth of modern telecommunication, oil and trade moguls. No matter, what country, city or region we are talking about, the richest or the poorest, socio-economic gap was much bigger than 10 years ago. Tiny oases of rich and ultrarich are surronded by ocean of poor or average people.

„The ranks of the world's billionaires, as monitored and tallied by our global wealth team, have yet again reached **all-time highs**. The 2013 Forbes Billionaires list now boasts 1,426 names, with an aggregate net worth of $5.4 trillion, up from $4.6

trillion. We found 210 new ten-figure fortunes. Once again the U.S. leads the list with 442 billionaires, followed by Asia-Pacific (386), Europe (366), the Americas (129) and the Middle East & Africa (103)." (Source „Inside The 2013 Billionaires List: Facts and Figures", published in Forbes, March 25, 2013). What 1,426 names mean in the world that count more than **7,111,850,855** people. So tiny population, so huge assets.

Looking at news, reports and articles in modern mainstream media, one gets an impression that in focus are rich and greedy, not poor and needy. Why journalists care more of powerfull than powerless people. Maybe, one out of ten articles, at best, deal with some sensistive issues of poor people; others peep to life of rich actors, directors, politicians and CEOs of big companies. So, we know more about Bentleys, Bayliners, new luxury appartments and love troubles of famous movie nad pop stars overseas than how many hungry children are in our community or city we live in. Does it mean that we don't care about poor people at all. To some extent yes. Media has assignment to sell stories to survive on „free market" not to solve social problems; that's on government.

Global mankind gravitates to one world, interconnected and linked to global village. Running away from the issue of rising gap between rich and poor and not protecting the poor could threaten the whole idea of globalism dramatically. The issue that there are more poor people not just in traditionally poor regions and countries, but even, in the West and OECD countries is something that needs immediate action. No any commonsense to have longer and longer list of ultrarich billionaires each new year, if number of poor rises. In „Global Pot" are not only countries like US, UK, Canada or Germany, that have, mainly, good standard of living, but extremely poor countries where people live on one dollar per day. In other words, they are somewhere on the line between life and death – starving, without money for medicaments, basic health care and education etc..

Therefore, authorities at all levels from community to country or region, must define precisely Basic Needs and resources to satisfy it. Basic Needs are primarily considered „Board and Lodging" (Food, Shelter and Clothing). In some countries (mainly western) that have long tradition of social assistance besides food, water, clothing and shelter some forms of sanitation, education and healthcare are included in term Basic Needs.

Namely, issue of Basic Needs is very arguable and depends on set of various elements. For example, meal for average and usually fat American or German is not the same as for Tibetan monk who can live several days on tea, or starving people in Africa and Asia. Nor quantity, neither the price of meal is the same. In Canada people on welfare were allowed to own car, which price didn't exceed $11,000. In many countries, as far as I know, even people who are full time employed cannot afford new car.

As we see, even term of Basic Needs is relative. Cars, personal electronic appliances such as TVs, camcorders and home theaters could be considered Basic Needs, although we can say that having no car, camcorder or bestseller novel is not necessary for survival. However, it should be solved by international teams of economists, statisticians, nutritionists, engineers and other experts. Maybe it sounds as utopia but not any single person life and survival on planet should be endangered by lack of means to satisfy Basic Needs.

No matter how poor country, or community is, one of main obligations of authorities should and must be to regulate area of social assistance and welfare of needy. Of course, it doesn't mean that government should cover all costs until getting University degree, but it must provide basic food, shelter and health care for poor and unlucky. It's really terrible seeing families sleeping in city parks or some tents at snowy weather - 15 degrees Centigrate, or searching for some thrown food in garbage, or let some people die, as simple as that, they had no money to pay for medicaments, which are not expensive for most population.

Excuses that there are no money due to budgetary restrictions sound ridiculous and cynical, in particular, in rich communities where live pretty good portion of well paid population earning more than $100,000 per year. US cannot show off with care of poor population, even in comparison to northern neighbor Canada, not to mention European countries that pay much more attention to poor and needy people. Not all European countries apply this type of solidarity; Scandinavian and Benelux countries have the best social assistance system. On the basis of mentioned statements one can conclude that United States belong to group of underdeveloped Third World countries, what, certainly, has nothing to do with real facts. Why is so? Probably, due to American tradition of "individualism" and neoliberalism, according to which, each single person takes responsibility for his or her life. That means - that government from community office to White House, is not appropriate address, at all, for any help if something goes wrong.

US politicians and government officials will rather debate North Korea or Kosovo issue, China economic threat or taxes on luxury yachts and hand made limousines than rise of welfare cheques for poor and unemployed. One gets an impression that is a shame to discuss publicly social assistance issue in America. On the other side, overseas, in Europe, many politicians are strongly devoted to defend and protect social assistance infrastructure when budgetary cuts are on agenda.

This issue is extremely important worldwide due to Third Industrial Revolution „jobicide" consequences that affect people, even, in most developed countries such is America, that was relied in last century, mainly, on unskilled labor of manual workers in factories. Many factory and office workers are directly replaced by robots and computers; class of average and slightly above average income workers are constantly sliding to welfare offices, not just for New Industrial Revolution, but for new Economic superpowers such as China, India or Brasil.

Therefore, social assistance issues must topped any political agenda no matter whether it's America, Europe, Russia, China or some other region. This is important for providing stable condidtions for social and economic development of any country, otherwise country will hold burden of conflicts, high criminal rates and event riots.

Besides, mentioned it's not shame to be humane, kind and solidary to poor, even if some attitudes and dogmas must be rethinked and revised. Finally, Mankind is, I guess, different from Wildlife, and people from animals, in particular, from beasts.

Berlin Wall Fall Legacy, Thinking or Sinking

For sure, as 1989 Berlin Wall Fall marked the end of communist era deep economic crisis today marks the end of US monopoly (not the end of capitalism as model).

But, even at the point of Wall Fall there were at least two different models of communist countries – Soviet and Yugoslavian. Western propaganda reduced all types to Soviet model for easing of breaking up that anachronistic system.

Abstraction is valid scientific tool, but in some cases could lead to wrong results. Certainly, putting aside Yugoslavian communist model was much more favorable for extensive western propaganda worldwide.

Each day bombing citizens with terms such as "Iron curtain", "dictatorship" etc, gradually resulted in World partition – Big West and the rest.

Berlin wall fall and breakup of former Socialist Federative Republic of Yugoslavia were finale of long term "Free world democracy" campaign against communism that was led and supported by USA.

Democracy defeated dictatorship. US "infinite race for getting rich ideology" put consumption "sui generis" as the top human priority. Perfectly organized and executed that propaganda is based on natural people dream of easy living.

Many people who was committed to fight for democracy 20 years ago, today feel betrayed. That feeling is intensified by negative effects of the worst global economic crisis in last 70 years. Twentieth Anniversary of communism fall coincides with the greatest global crisis in the world dominated by "free democratic capitalism".

Justification machinery turned on to make distance from "new revolutionary tendencies". Members of opposition parties are often called anarchists, populists, revolutionaries, words war getting on weight.

As Lenin said "No amount of political freedom will satisfy the hungry masses". There is no such good political marketing that will be accepted by fired people who lost their jobs.

Freedom versus survival - basic human choice. Hungry people are not even capable to feel the freedom, not to mention to enjoy and develop their personality in free environment.

People from former communist countries (Warsaw Pact, Yugoslavia, etc.) accustomed to 100 percent lifelong safety of job were pushed to neoliberal capitalism fighting at workforce market. Most of them were not brought up and trained for such working environment of absolute uncertainty. They have become bitter and deeply disappointed by democracy.

Step-by-step approach were skipped – "User friendly" transition to capitalism should be some form of mixture of socialism and social-democracy in early phase with dominant state control of economy, then second phase should be developed social-democracy with more intensive market laws, third logical phase is Keynesian economy with strong interventionist government policy. Governments, in this phase, use fiscal and monetary measures to mitigate the adverse effects of business cycles.

Finally, last phase is full free market neoliberal capitalism, with government serving and protecting capital.

If we have social stability in mind, I guess, none of former communist countries, which were less developed than old western countries, is not mature for neoliberal status.

Issue of freedom is relative. Majority of ordinary people would exchange freedom of criticizing politicians for good standard of living and job certainty. Even debating freedom issue -

Trite phrase that global crisis were made by "some bad and greedy guys of ours" has nothing to do with serious approach to solving extremely sensitive issue of huge accumulation of wealth of a very few, on one side, and fast impoverishment of majority population, on other side.

Even great economist John Maynard Keynes was wrong making forecasts in 1930, due to excessive relying on statistics at the same time neglecting human nature.

Accumulated capital has its own rules regardless social infrastructure in its environment. Instead of three hour shifts 5 days a week most of ordinary people afraid of job loss are in over timing. Keynes did not take in account that only very few will enjoy benefits of economic growth not majority of population.

"When the accumulation of wealth is no longer of high social importance, there will be great changes in the code of morals", Keynes said.

Unfortunately, accumulation of wealth has the highest social importance so far, and code of morals went for worse, not for better, If we could talk of any morals at all.

Once upon a time partnership reality between labor and capital as well as workers and management today turns utopia. Frankly, people today can freely speak on distant politicians, but not on their chiefs and CEOs. They lack that crucial relationship and partnership with their management structure. That can be illustrated as very busy crowded one way street.

In former Socialist Federative Republic of Yugoslavia labor organized workers` councils had great impact on managing boards, in some cases workers could have managed their CEOs dismissing.

In today's world labor is nothing more than, as simple as that, pure blotting pad of capital representatives decisions. Arisen modern dilemma is what brings higher profit rates and earnings – Permanent fear of job loss followed by miserable pay of majority of workers or partnership between labor and capital accompanied with better salaries of ordinary workers.

"Capital is reckless of the health or length of life of the laborer, unless under compulsion from society", Karl Marx said.

Neoliberal concept of global capitalism needs deep changes due to proving bad so far. Recent internet surveys show that more than 70 percent of population wish radical changes in corporate policy of pay range (decreasing huge bonuses etc..). Closing eyes won't go for better, government and society action is needed.

Maybe sticking back to Keynesian economics and principles of intervening would prove better than "going back to communism". If we address the issue properly and act in appropriate way, 30th or 40th Anniversary of Berlin Wall fall will not be shadowed by some new global crisis.

I guess that is the legacy of Berlin Wall Fall – Freedom, not only in philosophical and art terms, but, first of and after all, in **Economic Terms**, that means, more assets and higher standard of living for majority of people not a few selected ones.

There is upcoming celebration in 2014 of 25 year of Wall Fall. Quarter of century is quite enough time to show benefits of "Open Society, Free Market and Democracy" over „Iron Curtain". „Struggling for Survival Economy for Majority" is not in favor of mentioned, rather „Substitution of Iron Curtain with Economic Chains".

Divided versus uniform world

When I go back to 1982, when I earned my Bachelor Degree Diploma at The Faculty of Economics at Belgrade University, I always remember theme at the graduation exam titled „**The economic role in modern capitalism**". I was happy for I got best mark (10), and at that point, I guess, my work took all valid basic mainstream concepts and principles at that time. Frankly, I had not the slightest idea how our planet Earth would look like in 2013, neither most scientists and prophets knew that.

In 1982 the World was clearly politically divided to the West, the East and Non-aligned Third world. A few countries did not fit any group. Even countries in mentioned blocks have significant differences themselves. Country I live in, at that point, is marked as Communist single party political system with much more people freedoms than in China, Soviet Union and countries in Warsaw Pact. Yugoslavia is not attributed as country behind „iron curtain", but liberal, soft-core dictatorship with significant workers' rights to participate with management in company decision making process.

People from Warsaw Pact members were not allowed to travel abroad, for Yugoslavs it was even visa free for most countries, therefore term Freedom to travel wherever one wants" was strange to us. When I was 9-year old kid, I was in Dubrovnik with parents where we acquainted pair from Prague with daughter. They talked to us how many administrative obstacles and bureaucratic procedures people from Czechoslovakia had to pass to get a passport in order to come to two weeks vacation at

Adriatic coast. Most have never succeeded to pass the Czechoslovakia border. As a kid I had no idea what problems High Policy and Doctrines could have cause to average people who just wan to live an ordinary life, until my attending summer course of German language in East Berlin 12 years later. I saw divided town and divided people by high benchmark symbol of Cold War - Berlin Wall. Police patrol cars, wires and security cameras monitored access to the Wall. Many trying to reach West from East Berlin were killed next to the Wall.

I understood that East Germans were under Soviet occupation, brothers were separated from sisters, parents from sons and daughters. All on behalf and in the name of High Soviet Policy. Standing ten feet from the Wall I made out that there had not been any Freedom that would have been substituted for some vague Policy or Ideology. I was sad about ordinary people under Soviet dictatorship in all Warsaw Pact. „Face to Face" contact to Berlin Wall helped me to pay more attention to value of Freedom; I was happy and proud for Yugoslav citizenship. Our guide arranged one day trip to West Berlin, by underground. On a distance of, only, one underground stop different world – Great West, crowded with shops where you can see and buy (of course, just in case you can afford it) all what choosy consumer covets - various technical merchandise (TVs, gramophones), clothes, firearms etc.. I remember shop window with heavy Magnum handgun was priced at 400 marks. At that point „tourist attraction" in many western cities, so in West Berlin, was so called „peep show", where customers from small booths through glass hole had looked at nude girls dancing on podium. Rate was 1 Mark – 1 Minute. I didn't check but I guess that for more money one could have got more funs than a minute peep through small glass hole.

Exactly, as I had been taught at High School and Faculty of Economics at Belgrade University. On the West one can buy whatever he/or she wants if it is affordable. Consumption is Bible of the West, the stuff western people live and die for – The more you consume, the better you are, the better for government and whole community. Next lecture – Eastern Communist state run economy (Soviet model) is dogmatic without any serious attention to human consumption and personal needs. It means that Market values are totally neglected.

Yugoslavia was something in between as some cocktail – more freedoms and personal consumption than in Warsaw Pact but less than on the West.

Frankly, it was impossible to become rich although was easier to buy car, TV or travel abroad than in other Communist countries. I remember of words of, probably, most famous rock singer and musician Goran Bregovic, member of rock group „Bijelo Dugme", who said „I have bought new Jaguar, but I cannot buy friends".

People were not allowed to earn such amount of money to buy aircrafts, ships, factories. Taxation scissors had kept people not to stick out too much from crowd. Comparing that system to today's globalization is more like comparing different civilizations than systems. "People who once lived in Yugoslavia, Poland, Russia know it well—basic social values, economic relations, interpersonal communication, lifestyles, individual freedoms of thinking and moving were completely different.

Capitalist countries of European Community was one, Socialist countries of Warsaw Pact under Soviet Union was second, and Yugoslavia as independent socialist country was third entity. Each of three systems had its own rules different to rest of Europe and World.

That is not the case today. Once unskilled workers from Yugoslavia have gone to work in EC countries, mainly Germany. Highly industrialized countries of Western Europe had higher economic growth rate than rest of Europe (Yugoslavia and Warsaw Pact countries) and it was logical trend. People wish to live better. Today in one, united, fully linked and interconnected world we have reversible trend – One would normally expect fast-growing economies to attract migrant labor, not to send it. People from China, India, Brazil leave for North America and European Union, probably, due to expectations of higher wages than in countries of origin.

Next reversible trend is currency exchange rate fluctuation. When I have studied economics at Belgrade University I was taught that there were three main factors that affect exchange rate – Supply and demand of various currencies on market, Inflation rate and Balance of Payments.

Today, in economic reality, there is absolute domination of Supply & Demand Factor to others. For instance, Serbia has much higher inflation than EU countries which are significant foreign trade partners but exchange rate of Serbian currency

Dinar to Euro is, almost, at the same level as it was three years ago.

Another New Economic Rule in Global World – Inflation and Balance of Payments have impact to exchange rate. Result – No motivation for exports goods and services and permanently rising Huge Debt.

How it was earlier, in last century. If there is large deficit in Balance of Payments country currency is depreciated to make exports cheaper in order to decrease deficit and get rid off debts, in particular, huge debts.

At this point, in global world, countries are not independent in its economic policy. They cannot do with its country currency, credit and fiscal policy whatever they want. Their economic policy MUST BE coordinated and negotiated with Brussels, Washington and major financial organizations – IMF and World Bank. This, almost, ZERO independence, on long term, lead to DEBT SLAVERY. Continuous process of borrowing money without real possibilities to increase production makes all countries more and more heavily indebted.

„Bullshit, again Conspiracy theory", many would say. Is this someone's Top Priority – To make countries heavily indebted to manipulate and blackmail on behalf and in the name of spreading Democracy and Freedom worldwide.

But one could really doubt something goes in strange and suspicious way if some of the main economic principles that have been valid for more than 200 years were altered. Isn't it?

However, according to many reports, even rich Western countries, including US, are likely to continue suffering from increasing global competition—a trend that was intensified after Fall of Communism. United States of America and several traditional, rich countries of European Union will, likely, never be so dominant in economy as it was in divided world of 20th century.

Idea of Globalism and its spreading originated from America, probably to ensure higher standard of living for its citizens; but what can be expected at the end – Americans, in particular, people with average and lower income will be among biggest losers. Rising economies China, India, Russia and Brazil will, via „Free Market Economy Rules", impose fierce competition, lower wages and finally lower profits for rich and ultrarich.

This is metaphor of an old story of student who defeated his/her professor.

In this text, so far, mostly political divisions are reviewed, although, other types socio-economic, religious, ideological, even some sensitive life issues – sexual orientation or gun control, for instance, are very important. World global population is today, maybe, more sharply divided in mentioned fields and issues than in political sense.

Some would say „It's all about Politics". They are right to some extent, but this is nothing more or less than pure simplification of „hot life issues" of all of us ordinary people.

Is there anything where Americans are more divided than on issue of Gun Control. I guess, not. Freedom of Guns Possession versus People, in particular Kids Protection. More Americans were killed in mass and individual firearms shooting than in all wars from Vietnam to date taking together.

It wasn't enough to ban firearms sale to individuals. What should happen to please politicians to pass the law which will forbid firearms sale. It would be the right move aiming to minimize the risk of kids' murders. Kids lives should be and must be more important than Freedom of Firearms Possession.

But American Culture of having Firearms is so much in blood veins of most citizens that they would never give up their „pets", no matter how risky it is for them and their families and friends. According to Gallup support for stricter gun laws felt under 50 % in mid sixties last century with downward trend reaching record low 26 % in 2011. Americans, in general, have different attitudes on firearms than people in Europe and rest of the world.

I live in Serbia where one cannot acquire light firearms so easily; frankly, after break up of Yugoslavia and bloody civil war illegal light firearms trafficking has had upward trend. But in communist Yugoslavia (before break up) it was almost impossible to get a handgun without special permissions of state authorities. Result was country with almost zero homicide rate, at that point, one of most secure countries in the world.

However, this was one, maybe most drastic illustration how freedom and democracy could turn other way. I mean, are we allowed to put on risk lives of those (and their kids) 26 %, just for the sake majority (74 %) who oppose them. By exercising democratic and freedom routines, in such way, one becomes collaborator in potential murder. Politicians and all people who can influence our lives must be aware of it.

Or, maybe, they should be divided in order to live and work in different cities, communities, or even states where firearms sale would be strictly forbidden. I guess, it sounds more fair to those who are minority in this case.

I remember that once in communist Yugoslavia there were no such lunatics who had passion for mass shootings, criminal rate was, in general, very low. People were really afraid of Police at that time that was very brutal to any criminal, no matter whether criminal act had been murder, rape or burglary.

Efficient Police, ban of firearms and widespread fear of punishment may prevent criminals and lunatics from doing massacres.

Okay, do you advocate Single party Big Brother State Dictatorship? Of course NOT, but it is unsustainable to have such high rate of homicide. Those who lost someone of beloved – kids, parents, friends, for sure, think other way than those who think on this issue just in relations of "Firearms Possession Freedoms".

Back to Divided World? Maybe, Why not, if it would be make all of us happier and less frustrated. One Philosopher said - "Freedom and Democracy can be exercised by one unless others' rights are not threatened". I agree, that's true 100 %.

I picked up Gun Control as one of the hottest and most serious issues of living in modern world. There are numerous other issue such as Gay and Lesbian Rights, Right of Being Nude, Swingers Rights etc...

Think of some gay youngsters who committee suicide just for reason ambience they live in doesn`t accept such behavior. If they lived in Gay community **separated** from Straight people that would have not happened. Instead of suicides, mental and other illness or at least heavy frustrations they face" those people would be happy and productive citizens who could make significant contributions to whole society, not just community they live in.

Hmm, Is this Divided World so Perfect? Not at all, but in Transition period (that could last 10 to 15, or even 100 years) could be pretty good solution, although not so democratic.

How many times we have read in media on women who where arrested due to nude sunbathing on public beaches in some exotic countries where it is strictly forbidden. Many tourists are not acquainted with such facts - Muslim religion and tradition does not allow such behavior, it is very insulting. Such misunderstanding could even turn to diplomatic troubles. On the other side in Vrsar (Croatia) nudists are privileged – they can walk between bungalows and apartments, go to supermarket, hairdresser not just be nude on beach next to the sea.

There are hundred more nonpolitical and noneconomic issues that desperately need Version of Divided World that would meet standards of specific groups of people.

For example, conservative family oriented and playboys; why should I risk that somebody intercepts my spouse just for having fun. There would be less incidents and criminal rate would have been much lower in communities (cities) inhabited by people with similar attitudes. Next, more happy people could be more efficient at his workplace. That`s perfect – Nobody would oppose more efficient workers nor CEOs, neither Government (Federal or local, doesn`t matter). Of course, there won`t be „Iron Curtain" between such communities defined on specific needs of its citizens. Everybody can cross the „Border" any time he or she wants, but must have in mind that enters **different** community at his or her own responsibility.

That is not real Border with checkpoints, police and customs officers, just a place with noticeable, transparent signs that show potential commuters that they enter different people community, and must be aware of that fact.

Many will scream „That's not Democracy, That is Totalitarian isolationism".

No, Democracy is not forcing people to live other way they are accustomed to, either. In addition there is no „Iron Curtain", but imaginary border between such communities; that means free flows of people. Finally, this would be temporary solution unless all people (or most of them) do not realize that their freedom cannot threaten others freedom in any way.

But in some cases like Entering „Gun Free Zone" would be required temporary disposal of fire arms due to protecting freedom of those who choose to live without guns. Of course, after returning to "Gun Zone", firearms would be returned to owners at checkpoints.

Next, all people who decide to visit community where other rules are applied must be fully aware of different rules, otherwise they risk fines or even, imprisonment. For instance, they cannot walk nude in zone where is not allowed to.

It would be perfect to live in united, unique world, but insisting on that at any price, at this point, could make big troubles not just to small groups of people but whole countries, even regions with 180 degree different culture, tradition and religion. It must take step by step approach that could last for decades to achieve real not virtual harmony of the whole world. However, Force is not, in any case, the way to get united global world.

Some would say it is science fiction, utopia. Yes, everything new at the very beginning looks like utopia. What about first man in the Moon, or, maybe, high-speed Internet. What would be public, or even, experts and politicians opinion on mentioned issues a century ago.

At the end of this chapter - Back to political and economic division. What about population who would give up some percentage of economic standard and globalism ideals for calm living and working without threat of firing.

Forty years ago Yugoslavia was rather small but with very diversified production, maybe, a step for self-sufficiency. Frankly, space rockets and big passenger airplanes were not on production agenda, but almost all other merchandise yes. There were five motorcar factories, TV and Audio electronics as well as food and personal belongings factories. Merchandise met pretty high quality standards, people have bought domestic goods.

At that point there was no Globalism and Global Economic Competition of cheap production from Asia, in particular, China. There was no Unemployment too, Yugoslavian factories and economy was not forced to race with other countries at that time. Self-management Socio-economic system was unique and very specific; people were not frustrated by firing. It was more like living and working in a big community than in a sovereign independent country.

It is possible to make different type of economic and socio-political systems that will work as „entity sui generis" in order to meet various, specific needs and requirements of different group of people. There are many people today worldwide that would never exchange safety and harmony of living decent life for risk of survival and dreams of wealth. But, they have no any chance to do it.

Those Entities would work as small world for itself with lower, or sometimes, higher standards in some fields comparing to others. People living in such Mega Communities would fulfill their personal and professional ambitions due to competition protection from outside world, and, finally, they would be happy, not frustrated by forcing to accept something that is unacceptable for them.

Employment versus economic growth

Positive economic growth forecasts for 2010 could make wrong predictions in connection with employment rise. It applies to any other year 2014 or, maybe 2214, in socio-economic and political circumstances that exist nowadays. Media, experts, politicians, scientists and analysts, by purpose or accidentally doesn't matter, arouse vain hopes in public that employment will have growth too. The only expectations of average ordinary people are to get good and stable jobs. For sure, they are not interested in positive or higher percentage of economic growth, gross domestic product or higher output if it will not mean new working places.

Namely, there are two basic aspects of real outcome of economic growth. First, most frequent in common use in media and modern life is **statistical**. More goods & commodities produced and more services provided, according to statistical method, are quite enough to be happy about economy.

Yes, it would be valuable indicator of growth in industrial and pre-industrial age of capitalism. Nowadays, when labour is substitued by hi-tech equpment and tools positive figures could lead to wrong conclusions. Participation of labour comparing to capital invested in sophisticated machines is much lower today in postindustrial age than in industrial society.

Once upon a time we live in "labor intensive" economy; today in "capital intensive" with constant rising of domination of capital over labor. Trend is that relative proportion of labor (compared to capital) will be smaller in future. It means that production of new goods & commodities and providing services will need less workers (read human beings) than today.

Besides **statistical** there is second aspect of growth that is **real.**

Real aspect allows us to assign Quotation marks to word Growth.

Real aspect take in its consideration impact to real, ordinary people, workers, employees or human beings, doesn't matter.

Even the most naive optimists, not to mention serious scientists and experts, cannot predict higher part of labor in future. Unfortunately, from the view of ordinary people, that part will be much lower in next decades due to tremendous development of technology.

What is modern absurd, not just in theory but in real life too – is that we can have a many years with positive economic growth without a single worker employed (not to talk on some sharp employment rise). So most media, politicians and famous experts, in some way cheat us with positive digits in year 2010.

Labor, Capital and Government are crucial factors that affect any modern economy. Unfortunately, voting in favor of one or two of mentioned factors has been risk for putting in left (communist) or free market capitalist bloc.

One of the most famous economist of 20th century Milton Friedman opposed government regulation of economy. Among many his "antigovernment" quotes I will cite a striking one

"If you put the federal government in charge of the Sahara Desert, in 5 years there'd be a shortage of sand."

"History suggests that capitalism is a necessary condition for political freedom. Clearly it is not a sufficient condition". According to previous quote Friedman-economist has chosen capitalism as optimal system achieved so far.

Government "buffer zone" between necessary opponent factors Labor and Capital, in deep crisis time under the absolute rule of capitalism becomes "life boat" for the only socio-economic system remained.

Well, at this point we cannot take communist (socialist) system as something we deal with in real world. It is well known worldwide what are attribute of two communist countries remained (Cuba and North Korea). Most people would agree that taking in account such socio-economic system is not decent.

So, what is the way out? Probably, deep changes of global free market capitalism. Some will say that is sliding to the left, even to communism. For sure, that is not responsible acting which desperately needs new redesigned model of globally responsible capitalism.

Open minded people criticizing such neoliberal (no brakes) capitalism protect us from sliding to radical left ideas of state governed economy, one party democracy and banning private property over means of production.

Under high risk of, "quite new revolutionary ideas and so far unseen movements" that have optimal solutions for crisis, are developing countries of third world. In Africa, Asia, or Latin America soon we could face ideas of reducing multiparty system, freedom of speech even total nationalization of complete economy by state, in case we stick to "Bankers Driven Economy«, as Lord given.

Former French President Nicholas Sarkozy, no doubt, is not far left anarchist or communist but what he said in Davos Forum 2010 is warning to all of us.

"We are not asking ourselves what we will replace capitalism with, but what kind of capitalism we want?" Sarkozy said protecting capitalist model as the very best socio-economic system ever. On the other side French president has said "This capitalism has nothing to do with that we wanted to, so let`s change it".

"We must re-engineer capitalism to restore its moral dimension, its conscience," he said adding "By placing free trade above all else, what we have is a weakening of democracy".

Free trade and absolute power of "Bankers Economy" must be under some control. "There are remuneration packages that will no longer be tolerated because they bear no relation to merit, "Sarkozy said.

Politicians are angry with bankers who were marked as "Crisis Creators". We must have in mind that game is on capitalist politicians and capitalist bankers, so any arisen solutions, no matter how revolutionary are, will not threaten capitalist free market democratic framework.

Common sense shows that bankers have been stronger than politicians so far. Namely, it seems that bankers, not politicians, rule the world. Politicians fight bankers` bonuses blaming them for crisis. It would be perfect if bonuses were the only "crisis factors", the real problem might be deep in global socio-economic infrastructure.

Such focusing on bankers bonuses (if it was perfect in other fields) looks likes politicians` vanity and envy, not real assessment to crisis issue. "Killing Bonuses" method, is rather politicians` flirting with ordinary people in attempt to keep their voters than real solution to crisis issue.

However, deep changes of global capitalism are compulsory if we want to avoid more frequent and more severe economic crisis in future.

New Economic Order Stereotype Slogans

I wonder can we get away from foggy slogans. Each Time, System, Period has its own original slogans we are supposed to believe as if they are Axioms.

When I was young I have lived in Socialist Federal Republic of Yugoslavia dominated by single Communist party headed by globally known politician at that time Josip Broz Tito, who was longlife president of the country too. His favorite and, probably, most frequently used slogan was **HUMAN BEING IS OUR BIGGEST WEALTH**. That Quote had widespread use in all Republics - Serbia, Slovenia, Croatia, Bosnia, Montenegro and Macedonia (today, independent countries), in all companies, government institutions…People were expected to act in that manner. Ordinary people, in particular, workers in so called Organizations of Associated Labor (term for Company), government institutions etc…It was something as God Commandment, Quote from local Yugoslavian Bible (Program of League of Communists of Yugoslavia). Point was that Human and his or/and good is sense of all activities in society and state. Bottom line was that People were supposed to work, first of all, for benefit of all community, not for selfish individual, private interests.

By Fall of Communism people were used to think that such foggy Slogans that really meant nothing (or almost nothing), but political and ideological spinning, had flown to the history forever.

Unfortunately, they were terribly wrong. These days we face New Quotes that fit New Rules and Order and are intended for modern population. Once again, it's confirmed that each concept, religion or/and ideology has its own „Brainstorming Proverbs", no matter how democratic system is.

If you succeed escaping reading or listening to Bible or Communist Party Manifesto messages, it doesn't mean you are „Brainwashproof", at all.

New Globalist Economy, New Economic Order and finally „New Holy Slogans".

There is a bunch of them, most of them are boring and not understandable to most of world population, in spite of that, they are intended to be 100 percent clear to all.

In this chapter, I`ll focus and try to analyze a couple, or so, of, maybe, most common and most frequent modern time slogans.

REDUCING DEBT, probably the most frequent Holy Slogan today. There is, almost, no single day, that issue is not mentioned in mainstream and local media worldwide. Politicians, CEOs, scientists, kings, singers, low ranked office and factory workers ordinary people in the streets, even homeless and drunk men in restaurants and coffee bars speak on debt crisis. There is almost no person on the face on the Earth who is not heavily pressed by global debt crisis. Next, if we take **REDUCING DEBT** as the very main slogan, we can outline many subcategories derived from that Holy Quote, such as budget cuts, reducing public debt, reducing human resources costs (what usually means firing), less assets to health, education and social service, that consequently leads to next Holy Slogan **PRIVATIZATION OF PUBLIC SERVICES.** One of ways to get rid off debts is to sell public services to private persons. International Monetary Fund, World Bank, bunch of presidents, kings, prime ministers, Nobel prize winners, economists, mainstream global, regional, and even local media talk the same sentences each single day. Average man, would say „Wise people, they must be right". So, message is - Go on and Privatize (sell) all you can, hospitals, schools, state real estate assets, etc...Government will erase debts, everything will be fixed when ALL ASSETS come to PRIVATE hands and all people will be happy and fully (or almost fully) employed. It sounds perfect. But, is that so in real life.

Third, modern „mind killing" slogan is **COMPETITION**. We can hear broadcasted messages from VIPS „Let Competition, then all be fixed in short term", „Just, provide terms and conditions for perfect competition, monopolies will disappear, prices will go down, and consumers would be happy buying more goods and services". Well, I would say, put one finger on your head, snap fingers on another hand and remember „Alice in Wonderland", magical story for children. Who is Alice in this „Slogans Case"? Probably, ordinary people, who are supposed to swallow and digest any wisdom they hear from New World Order Missionaries.

If **COMPETTITION,** per se, can solve all (or almost all) problems caused by monopolies why prices go high to the sky even in countries which economies are not dominated by monopolies or oligopolies, but network of various producers and distributors, that are, under assumption, in „fierce market competition".

Let's take in considerations some statistical and mathematical aspect of term **COMPETITION**. There are TWO main sides of COMPETITION – On one side there is Competition between big production and distribution companies, banks owned by a very few extremely rich people called tycoons. That kind of Competition is frequently analyzed, studied and reported, on daily basis, in Media, particular mainstream media, that run as "Six speed Brainwashing Machines". Another side of Competition is more like „Survival among the beasts in Wild life" than a classic Competition modus. That is Competition between among all other people, except ultrarich - employed, underemployed, unemployed, skilled workers and workers performing unskilled simple labor; employees with University degree diplomas etc... On the Earth live more than 7,000,000,000 people; at its best not more than 20,000 people, could be included on first side of ultrarich – company owners, show business megastars, kings, presidents and prime ministers. They are very, very rich and influential and all can be placed in some bigger shopping mall. What about another side – other 7,000,000,000 ordinary average, poor and starving people. You, for sure, must admit that it is really big group of extremely different people who cannot be organized in any way in reality due to logic of Big Figures (7,000,000,000 versus 20,000). Another problem is Wealth, that means their influence is close to zero.

That is not the case with first group of very wealthy who are, often, member of governments, monarch families, owners of big companies, or, at least, have close ties with them. They prefer negotiations instead of competition. They NEGOTIATE, not FIGHT the PRICE. Better definition is term PARTNERSHIP than COMPETITION.

Those selected ones usually choose some exotic destination in 7 star resort, far away from media cameras and microphones. It is some kind of „covert mission". WHY ?

Public – workers and ordinary people, as well as political establishment, ask for COMPETITION, not NEGOTIATIONS. Despite that public will tycoons DO NOT like wasting their resources (money, time, energy...) on such hazards as open and fierce Competition.

Therefore, it is not real to expect that COMPETITION will solve all problems and bring ORDINARY, AVERAGE PEOPLE to Paradise. It`s more likely that such way of acting will decrease price 1 to 2 per cent, at the same time reducing wages 10 to 20 percent of ordinary workers, than vice-versa. Those 20,000 worldwide can articulate common interest, even form Interest Group, other 7,000,000,000 cannot do it, due to various limitation factors (three of which I mentioned in previous paragraphs – LOGIC OF BIG NUMBERS, WEALTH and INFLUENCE).

However, bottom line is - that COMPETITION is just one more fairy tale for modern adults.

All mentioned and, many other similar new slogans, are injected, directly through funnels of media, particular mainstream, directly into our brains. Most of „Mainstream" politicians, scientists, experts, „Frequent winners of reputable international prizes and rewards", even „artists in charge" (independent from own thinking) would say – That's ridiculous, Conspiracy Theory, lie or bullshit.

Yes, they are right, if we look at such Holy Quotes as Messages from Big Brother.

US President Barack Obama has said five years ago that this economic crisis is the worst since great depression in 1930s. Approximately, at the same time BBC conducted global online survey on debt crisis. Result was – More than 70 per cent of people worldwide asked for radical changes in economy, particular regarding more fair distribution of income between rich and poor. What happened half decade later – NOTHING. Rich are still very rich, poor stayed poor.

All, Media, Politicians, VIPs and other influential factors and elements, are used only as recording devices and transmitters to crowds, or more politely, masses, without any serious movement to substantial and fundamental changes of current socio-economic structure of the World. Maybe, they do not know to do it, or, as simple as that, they are not allowed to. Okay, it's high time to stop this digression from main topic in this chapter, and return to **Reducing Debt** (public, foreign or budgetary).

Please, first look at table below. Sustainable Net debt is (60% of GDP). Each figure over 60 percent shows that country is indebted.

Country	Debt % GDP	Year		Read More	
1	Japan	229.8	2011	IMF	Japan
2	Greece	163.3	2011	IMF	
3	Jamaica	139.0	2011	IMF	
4	Lebanon	136.2	2011	IMF	
5	Eritrea	133.8	2011	IMF	
6	Italy	120.1	2011	IMF	Italy
7	Barbados	117.3	2011	IMF	
8	Portugal	106.8	2011	IMF	Portugal
9	Ireland	105.0	2011	IMF	Ireland
10	United States	102.9	2011	IMF	US
11	Singapore	100.8	2011	IMF	
12	Iceland	99.2	2011	IMF	
13	Belgium	98.5	2011	IMF	
14	Mauritania	92.4	2011	IMF	
15	Côte d'Ivoire	90.5	2011	IMF	
16	Iraq	86.9	2011	IMF	
17	Grenada	86.6	2011	IMF	
18	France	86.3	2011	IMF	France
19	Canada	85.0	2011	IMF	Canada
20	United Kingdom	82.5	2011	IMF	UK
21	Bhutan	82.0	2011	IMF	

22	Germany	81.5	2011	IMF	
23	Hungary	80.4	2011	IMF	
24	Belize	80.3	2011	IMF	
25	Sri Lanka	79.0	2011	CIA	
26	Cape Verde	77.6	2011	IMF	
27	Egypt	76.4	2011	IMF	
28	Israel	74.3	2011	IMF	
29	Sudan	73.1	2011	IMF	
30	Austria	72.2	2011	IMF	
31	Guinea	72.2	2011	IMF	
32	Nicaragua	72.0	2011	IMF	
33	Cyprus	71.8	2011	IMF	
34	Malta	70.9	2011	IMF	
35	Zimbabwe	70.3	2011	IMF	
36	Dominica	69.9	2011	IMF	
37	Jordan	69.8	2011	IMF	
38	The Gambia	68.8	2011	IMF	
39	Spain	68.5	2011	IMF	Spain
40	India	68.1	2011	IMF	
41	Netherlands	66.2	2011	IMF	
42	Brazil	66.2	2011	IMF	
43	Guyana	61.8	2011	IMF	
44	Pakistan	60.1	2011	IMF	
45	Sierra Leone	60.0	2011	IMF	

46	Albania	58.9	2011	IMF	
47	Poland	55.4	2011	IMF	
48	Morocco	54.4	2011	IMF	
49	Uruguay	54.2	2011	IMF	
50	Fiji	53.9	2011	IMF	
51	Malaysia	52.6	2011	IMF	
52	Kyrgyz Republic	52.4	2011	IMF	
53	El Salvador	50.8	2011	IMF	
54	Mauritius	50.6	2011	IMF	
55	Belarus	50.2	2011	IMF	
56	Norway	49.6	2011	IMF	
57	Kenya	48.9	2011	IMF	
58	Switzerland	48.6	2011	IMF	
59	The Bahamas	48.6	2011	IMF	
60	Finland	48.6	2011	IMF	
61	Serbia	47.9	2011	IMF	
62	Slovenia	47.3	2011	IMF	
63	Denmark	46.4	2011	IMF	
64	Montenegro	45.8	2011	IMF	
65	Croatia	45.6	2011	IMF	
66	Venezuela	45.5	2011	IMF	
67	Slovak Republic	44.6	2011	IMF	
68	Tanzania	44.4	2011	IMF	

69	Myanmar	**44.3**	2011	IMF
70	Argentina	**44.2**	2011	IMF
71	Mexico	**43.8**	2011	IMF
72	Ghana	**43.4**	2011	IMF
73	Malawi	**42.5**	2011	IMF
74	Tunisia	**42.4**	2011	IMF
75	Thailand	**41.7**	2011	IMF
76	Czech Republic	**41.5**	2011	IMF
77	Central African Rep.	**40.9**	2011	IMF
78	Taiwan	**40.8**	2011	IMF
79	Bosnia – Herzegovina	**40.6**	2011	IMF
80	Senegal	**40.6**	2011	IMF
81	Philippines	**40.5**	2011	IMF
82	Turkey	**39.4**	2011	IMF
83	Lithuania	**39.0**	2011	IMF
84	South Africa	**38.8**	2011	IMF
85	Vietnam	**38.0**	2011	IMF
86	Panama	**37.8**	2011	IMF
87	Latvia	**37.8**	2011	IMF
88	Sweden	**37.4**	2011	IMF
89	Ethiopia	**37.3**	2011	IMF
90	New Zealand	**37.0**	2011	IMF

91	Ukraine	36.5	2011	IMF	
92	Bahrain	36.5	2011	IMF	
93	Tajikistan	35.3	2011	IMF	
94	Burundi	35.3	2011	IMF	
95	Armenia	35.1	2011	IMF	
96	Colombia	34.7	2011	IMF	
97	Korea	34.1	2011	IMF	
98	Nepal	34.1	2011	IMF	
99	Bangladesh	33.9	2011	CIA	
100	Georgia	33.9	2011	IMF	
101	Hong Kong	33.9	2011	IMF	
102	Mozambique	33.2	2011	IMF	
103	Romania	33.0	2011	IMF	
104	Bolivia	32.9	2011	IMF	
105	Chad	32.2	2011	IMF	
106	Rep. Congo	32.0	2011	IMF	
107	Qatar	31.5	2011	IMF	
108	Benin	31.3	2011	IMF	
109	Angola	30.9	2011	IMF	
110	Costa Rica	30.8	2011	IMF	
111	Mali	30.6	2011	IMF	
112	Burkina Faso	29.4	2011	IMF	
113	Dominican Republic	29.3	2011	IMF	
114	Uganda	29.2	2011	IMF	

115	Cambodia	28.6	2011	IMF	
116	Honduras	28.1	2011	IMF	
117	Macedonia	28.1	2011	IMF	
118	Zambia	26.1	2011	IMF	
119	China	25.8	2011	IMF	
120	Indonesia	25.0	2011	IMF	
121	Guatemala	24.1	2011	IMF	
122	Rwanda	23.4	2011	IMF	
123	Moldova	23.4	2011	IMF	
124	Australia	22.9	2011	IMF	
125	Solomon Islands	22.6	2011	IMF	
126	Republic of Congo	22.2	2011	IMF	
127	Namibia	21.9	2011	IMF	
128	Peru	21.6	2011	IMF	
129	Luxembourg	20.8	2011	IMF	
130	Suriname	20.6	2011	IMF	
131	Gabon	20.5	2011	IMF	
132	Niger	18.9	2011	IMF	
133	Ecuador	18.0	2011	IMF	
134	Nigeria	17.9	2011	IMF	
135	Swaziland	17.5	2011	IMF	
136	Botswana	17.3	2011	IMF	
137	Bulgaria	17.0	2011	IMF	

138	United Arab Emirates	**16.9**	2011	IMF
139	Turkmenistan	**15.4**	2011	IMF
140	Liberia	**13.9**	2011	IMF
141	Paraguay	**13.7**	2011	IMF
142	Cameroon	**12.9**	2011	IMF
143	Iran	**12.7**	2011	IMF
144	Kazakhstan	**10.9**	2011	IMF
145	Haiti	**10.6**	2011	IMF
146	Azerbaijan	**10.2**	2011	IMF
147	Algeria	**9.9**	2011	IMF
148	Chile	**9.9**	2011	IMF
149	Russia	**9.6**	2011	IMF
150	Uzbekistan	**9.1**	2011	IMF
151	Equatorial Guinea	**8.4**	2011	IMF
152	Saudi Arabia	**7.5**	2011	IMF
153	Kuwait	**7.3**	2011	IMF
154	Estonia	**6.0**	2011	IMF
155	Madagascar	**5.7**	2011	IMF
156	Oman	**5.1**	2011	IMF

Sources:

- CIA factbook – National debt by Country
- Public debt, International Monetary Fund, April 2012
- Eurostat pdf.

If you add personal and public debt together, both government loans and private loans, credit card debts and mortgages, the results are a little different. The total amount owed to parties outside the country is called 'external debt'. The top ten most indebted countries in the world by external debt looks like this:

1. United States – $13,703,567 million
2. United Kingdom – $10,450,000
3. Germany – $4,489,000
4. France – $4,396,000
5. Netherlands – $2,277,000
6. Ireland – $1,841,000
7. Japan – $1,492,000
8. Switzerland – $1,340,000
9. Belgium – $1,313,000
10.   Spain – $1,313,000

Great surprise, all countries are rich highly industrialized. What about Third world poor countries? Figures above are just absolute indicators. They do not show us how big economy output is. Although American GDP is enormous US is in group of heavily indebted countries. Not all of the countries with extremely high debt relative to their GDPs are doing poorly. Government debt of Germany and Japan is high, but these countries can afford it. Their high debt-to-GDP ratios are balanced by relatively strong economies and wealthy populations. Germany has the highest GDP in Europe and the fourth highest in the world. While Japan's economy was derailed by the earthquake and resulting nuclear tragedy, it remains the third-largest economy by GDP.

This chart above shows that US has significantly higher Per

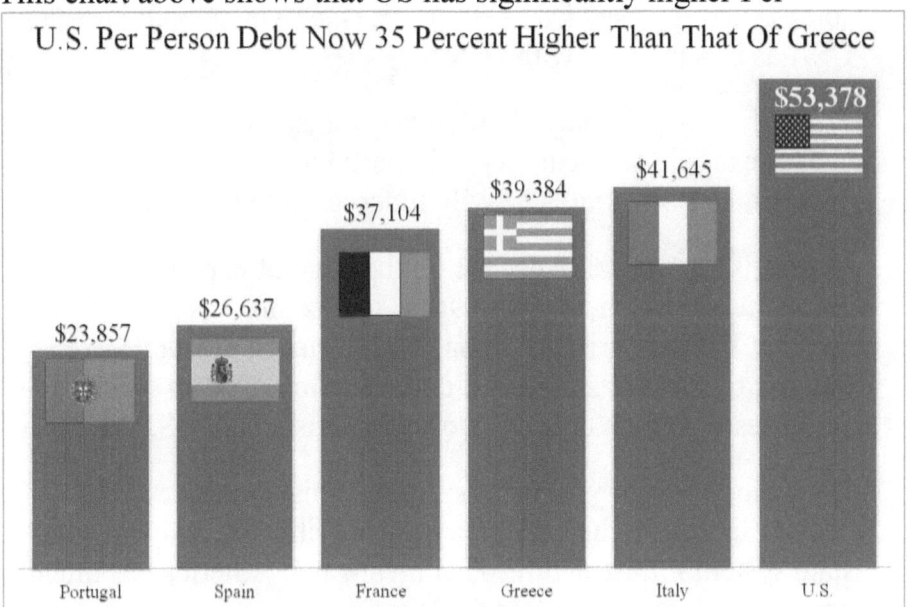

U.S. Per Person Debt Now 35 Percent Higher Than That Of Greece

Portugal $23,857
Spain $26,637
France $37,104
Greece $39,384
Italy $41,645
U.S. $53,378

Source: Senate Budget Committee Ranking Member Jeff Sessions' Republican staff calculations of data from the IMF and 2013 Budget Summary Tables. Updated with 2012 Population and General Government Gross Debt in national currency; currency conversions are based on Dec. 31, 2011 euro to dollar conversion rates. General Government Gross Debt includes federal, state, and local debt, but excludes intragovernmental holdings. Under President Obama's FY 2013 Budget, U.S. gross federal debt per person would reach $75,000 by 2022.

Person Debt than Greece, Portugal and Spain. "The disparity between per capita debt in the U.S. and Greece has grown 40 percent (roughly $8,400) since 2011. Now, U.S. per person debt is 35 percent higher than that of Greece, and is also higher than per capita debt in Portugal, Italy, or Spain (which together with Greece make up the so-called PIGS countries)," according to International Monetary Fund report.

Okay, why the Greeks are under so intensive pressure to cut debt? Greek economy is much weaker than American (see relative figures in table above). Debt to GDP ratio is much more in favor of US. That is purely ECONOMIC reason, but is there some other, let's say POLITICAL reason, why nobody threatens USA as it is the case with Greece.

Probably, yes. Although Debt issues are economic matters, we cannot exclude political factor, in particular, if we address Debt problem in USA, that is heavily indebted country too.

Greece is almost half a decade on the edge of expelling from eurozone, despite heavy protests in that country. Nor a single day that EU debt crisis is among top stories in media. However, judging by articles in various, particular mainstream media, EU countries are much deeper involved in crisis than US. How that?

US is single country – single system – single currency and besides that, still, the only superpower with coherent, compact state system infrastructure. That means that America has much greater chances to survive the Debt Crisis.

That doesn't apply to European Union countries, that have SINGLE currency – Euro, but different, incoherent and often incompatible fiscal systems. If EU was one country (not Union of various countries) chances for Debt Crisis coming out would be significantly better.

At this point, with several countries waiting in queue for access to full membership, and group of traditional EU members in deep debt crisis, it is unrealistic to expect higher degree of integration, in particular, in short and mid term.

North and South America, Russia, China and India (BRICS countries) face more favorable conditions regarding "Crisis Exit Rate" due to much „lower cohesion".

Should we smash computers and/or CEOs

It was hot summer of 1997 when I bought my first personal computer. Pentium PC at 166 MHZ with hard disc 3.2 GB, 32 MB EDO RAM and 4 MB graphic card was, at that point, best home model on Serbian PC consumers market and, of course, rather expensive (approximately 2,700 $ with monitor and ink jet printer). Bulky seventeen inches monitor had almost 25 kilos. After connecting all cables and installing all necessary software I have started working at this „magic hi-tech gadget". Frankly, It was not my first experience with PC, I have worked in my office for seven years with similar machines (not so sophisticated models - 386 and 486 dx with Black-white monitor). Connecting and using available information at Internet was primary goal those „revolutionary days". Phone bills tripled due to use of dial up modem for linking to World Wide Web. Some family members were not happy about that. Downloading and uploading at speed of 33.6 kbps was like „riding on snails".

Nowadays, ultra-high Internet speeds are more than 1,000 faster than 16 years ago. However, I was astonished by my PC performance. Global, fast, efficient and cheap communication via electronic mail was something that impressed me most at the very beginning of my personal friendship with PC. On the day of sending first email via World Wide Web was something like „Revolution in communication". It was one of a very few, several, historic days in my life. I felt thrilled, how technology can make people lives in positive way. Several clicks by mouse substitutes at least one hour of spare time. No need, any more, to go to the nearest post office to buy envelopes and stamps, to wait in queue, in front of traffic lights for green...It seemed really fantastic to me those days. Unfortunately, Internet was not so much widespread in Serbia at that time. Country was terribly exhausted by UN sanctions and civil war caused by break up of Socialist Federative Republic of Yugoslavia. Most people could not afford to buy home computers, I used to buy 5 to 10 hours Dial up for my purposes. I shared my first experience of using internet with some of my friends. I expected positive reactions, but I was wrong. Good friend of mine, who was economist too, as I am, started fierce criticism of my attitudes. „What kind of man you are, do you happen to know how many people will be fired ?", he said. I did not need much time to make out my friend was right. On the other side, I felt ashamed relying on easiness, not taking in consideration economic consequences.

Today, in year 2013, computers and hi-tech gadgets are fully integrated to our business, as well as private lives. Mobile phones are small computers more powerful than firs PC. Even housewives are forced to learn some basics of programming in order to operate laundry machines. Frankly, it is not so sophisticated and complex as designing large database of bank clients, but it's not enough to push couple of buttons as our mothers and grandmothers used to do. Some old and retired journalist envy their young colleagues who, simply mark and delete unnecessary sentences and paragraphs, inserting proper ones at same blank space, without getting angry frequently pulling paper out of old fashioned typewriter and inserting new one, just for one wrong sentence.

Can we, just, imagine at what ease and speed such writers as Mark Twain, Ernest Hemingway or Norman Mailer would create their novels if they had computers and internet. They could keep control and fix their private lives to less painfully, in other words, chances to be happy would have been much bigger, they would not be so frustrated with art. Finally, we could read today at least doubled number of masterpieces.

Norman Mailer as unknown author simultaneosly offered same book manuscript to 18 different publishing house. It looks like this without New Technology – One original should be copied to 18 manuscripts in some store.

All copies should be bound with cover pages for Publisher viewing. Author must make many phone calls to set appointment to each of 18 publishers. Finally, he goes from one to another (it might me that all publishers are not located in the same city) to hand manuscript. It could take days, or even weeks.

Okay, let's involve computer technology in mentioned operations – all work could be executed in front of computer sitting in comfortable armchair, clicking mouse and sending e-mails to different publishers e-mail addresses. What is, maybe, most important is that all job can be done within 24 hours or less. Really great saving of time we all desperately need, isn't it.

Everything looks much faster, easier and more comfortable to do. So, What's Wrong then? Why should anybody oppose computers in our economy and lives?

Yes, everything is perfect until we take in consideration Human Resources and Human Cost of Computer Technology Expansion.

Then, Should we turn Luddites, who were destroying new machines at the very beginning of 19th century in the era of British industrial revolution. Luddites had thought that machines had been responsible for job loss and decreasing wages. Workers at that time considered machines as main enemy to them.

Machinery was wrecked, mills were burned down and the Luddites fought pitched battles with the British Army. The response of the state was brutal. Machine breaking became a capital offence. The Court Verdict for one smaller group of Luddites was Death Penalty that was executed by hanging, others were transported to Australia. State did not allow that Luddites become country spread movement. Since then, there were no similar attempts with such „concept" that has made any significant and respectful moves to „Eliminating New Technology".

On the contrary, New Technology has become gradually more popular to all groups and classes, rich, average, poor, CEOs, workers, employed and even unemployed...It doesn't sound logically. Why should people be „friendly" to computers if it replace humans. No easy answer...It is not the first time people face impact of introducing New Technology. The Third Industrial Revolution has just been in progress. Two Industrial Revolutions are far behind us.

The newest Industrial Revolution has some specific characteristic comparing to previous two. First, it takes place in new global world that is not so divided as it had been during first two revolutions, in particular, The Second Revolution.

Our Planet was clearly and sharply divided in last century by „iron curtains" of political and ideological systems of communist and democratic multiparty countries. Results of those divisions were catastrophic – Two World Wars in period shorter than four decades. Great Depression was ended by Second World War and more than 50,000,000 dead, mainly, in Europe and Russia.

The Second Industrial Revolution has taken part in extremely unfavorable circumstances. It doesn't mean that this deep economic crisis that last for six year and which many compare to 1929 Great Depression will end with World War. One, global, interconnected World, some call „Global Village" is perfect barrier to extremist ideas. This era of global internet and telecommunications enables access to information and data to average and ordinary people who will never allow again anybody to manipulate them. Fascism, Stalinism or any extremism or totalitarian system seems totally unreal at this level of technological and communications progress.

So, political & ideological divisions are much more favorable for the ongoing Third Industrial Revolution. Therefore, possibility of new World war as a way of solving conflict is much more theory than realistic option.

However, partial regional conflicts and local wars are inevitable, even, during The Third Industrial Revolution. The newest Third industrial revolution has best chance to be the smoothest so far. There are no serious political and ideological barriers and obstacles, no walls and "iron curtains" that cannot be break through and put aside by telecommunications and internet tools. It looks perfect, isn't it.

Unfortunately, each New Technology and Industrial Revolution was, at its early stage, "Job killing", in particular, latest that use computer and robots who replace vast number of humans. Steam engines locomotive fired by coal once were replaced by electricity driven trains, train operator has remained, but man who feed steam engine by coal was fired. Train crews were halved.

What's going on with workers today? Computer controlled Robotic arms on routine simple jobs at car assembly line replace not one or couple, but dozens of workers who perform unskilled labor. Number of replaced workers is big even in the case of skilled labor (college and University degree employees). Computers are faster and faster each single day, business software more efficient and "user friendly", and corporate headquarters offices are worldwide less populated than ever so far. Employment offices are full of uneducated as well as University degree unemployed people who search their way to success. CEOs and managers weigh costs relying more and more often on computers, not on humans. Hi-tech machines are so good, they don't use holidays, sick or maternity leave, they do not object anything, work the same way and efficiency in first and eighth hour.

Bosses do not need to negotiate wages and other sensitive issues with robots and computers. Put yourself in their shoes, more efficient computer guided sophisticated machines are, as simple as that, more „cooperative" and, finally, better „workers" than humans. So it's logic principle – more hi-tech machines, less employed humans. There is permanent process of increasing speed and overall performance of new computer models and machines based on that technology...What can be expected in the near future; some experts predict that within several decades computers and robots will be „sole thinking machines" that would control itself by itself. It means that even employees who work complex jobs today, or low rank, or maybe middle ranked managers will be fired in that case. Unemployment could reach 90 percent even in high developed countries, should we play hide-and seek wide shut eyes and say what can we do about it. Is that sustainable at all.

Luddites would say „Take hammers and start crashing computers they kill our jobs and us". More dangerous idea of political and ideological extremists is that „Machines should not be blamed for unemployment, but people". „People, specific group (CEOs, managers, owners, bosses, shareholders) introduce computers in production, machines are not teleported from unknown location to our offices and assembly, production lines. Therefore, rebellion must be against them, not computers".

Does it mean Revolution with all horrible consequences?!? For sure, I wouldn't advocate such way of solving problems, but tremendous technological progress desperately needs new appropriate Social infrastructure, otherwise our planet would pocket of ever rising and unpredictable conflicts with immense repercussions.

Jeremy Rifkin the author of The New York Times best selling book, The Third Industrial Revolution, How Lateral Power is Transforming Energy, the Economy, and the World says that *„The Third Industrial Revolution makes possible a new Distributed Social Vision in the 21st century. Most citizens of the world, when asked what they most hope for, say they envision a good "quality of life". The dream of quality of life emphasizes individual opportunity, social and human rights, balancing the social and market models, and building bridges of cooperation and peace. Underlying this expansive new 21st century social vision is the commitment that millions of people share to create a just and sustainable society for their children and future generations".*(quotation from „Leading the Way to the Third Industrial Revolution and a New Distributed Social Vision for the World in the 21st Century" By Jeremy Rifkin).

It's inevitable as a „Free Fall Law" in physics that all Industrial and Economic Revolutions were followed by significant, substantial Political and Social changes (in some cases real revolutions).

Maybe, government at all levels, from community to state and regional, should be the „middle man" between ordinary workers and unrestricted will of CEOs and rich. New Technology cannot be harmful to 90 percent of people and good for one tenth or even less. Powerful individuals who can influence global world must have in mind that no technology so far in human history has so dramatic degree of human replacement as it has been with Computer Technology.

Globalization of Third Industrial Revolution is particularly painful for those parts of Globe where Second Industrial Revolution is in its beginning, or mid-age. It applies to many African and Asian countries whose people live in extreme poverty without education and health care system, where unemployment rate is much higher than in developed countries. In other words, they skip Second Industrial Revolution sinking in Third Industrial Revolution often not by their own will. They were given laptops and new modern android mobile phones even they have not be accustomed to use usual electric appliances in proper way that were used in the West half a century ago.

Doing this way this poor and uneducated people get more frustrated and unhappy. Nobody decent, can expect from such people to get IT college or university degree „overnight", immediately, in particular, if they even barely can write. Exercising „globalist style economy" this way is real risk to turn such people extremists and antiglobalists. That's unpredictable negative effect of „enforced speedy globalisation process". This could turn to serious conflicts and social unrests, in particular, in areas that are dominated by different religion, culture and tradition than in „Western Flaghip Globalisation Countries."

Next, those countries are usually with very high unemployment rate and if similar procedure of introducing High technology makes record high unemployment even in G20 countries, consequences in poor countries could be disastrous.

If Globalism is wanted as „The Newest Ideology of World" to be accepted and adopted by all mankind, it must be revised, in particular, regarding the way and pace of spreading it to poor countries where is high „inherited" unemployment rate as recidive from previous Industrial Revolutions. Otherwise, there is real threat of fierce and intensive Antiglobalist movements in mentioned countries and regions. And, unfortunately, they were given perfect alibi to uprise against globalism, that would be blamed for all economic evil even for troubles that were inherited much earlier when globalism had been just theoretical thesis.

These extremist views regarding role of globalism could be, in a way, some kind of new Luddites, but destruction, now, is not aimed to machines (computers), but other people. Nobody is protected, from class of poor to managers, CEOs and high ranked politicians. From isolated criminal acts of individuals and isolated groups to organized bounty could be just few steps. They are aware that computers are not truth cause of their poor social status, but people who produce and introduce them to factories, offices and homes. And they are absolutely right; maybe in the future, at higher scientific and technological degree of development, let's say after The Fourth Industrial Revolution – when sole thinking robots and machines will make up their decisions at its own without any human help, machines should be blamed for all problems. At this point, it has nothing to do with common sense.

Introducing high technology must be tailored on concrete measures for each society, country or region, otherwise it's very bed marketing for globalization trend. We must remember that widespread industrialization and access and availability of various consumers' merchandise such as cameras, TVs and cars was „differentia specifica" of Capitalism versus Communism. Besides Freedom of Thought and Moving, Travelling it was one of „Aces" that substantially helped defeat of Communism.

It's not logic that Globalism (read Global Capitalism) with such tradition in synchronized activity with science & technological progress cannot cope with it in Third Industrial Revolution. Frankly, this Postindustrial Capitalism is much more careless than its predecessor that had "competitor" in Communism.

However, I must use a neologism „jobicide" for newest computer and robot based technology. Of course, this applies to uncontrolled, unadjusted and linear introduction of mentioned machines.

It is not overestimate comparing rate and degree of human force replacement by computers to those during First and Second Industrial Revolution is as if comparing one islolated murder or victims of serial killers to Genocide. Well, should we get rid of any scientific & technological progress and let it to some autistic lunatics to waste their time. Of course, Not... Therefore,

Employment Issue must be essentially revised and set as the Highest Priority and the most sensitive issue on agenda of politicians and other known and unknown persons who make our World going this way.

That dirty word Class

In English language term „Four letter words" usually marks dirty, obscene words used for or/and linked to some sexual activity. According to frequency of use in media, particular mainstream, in past two decades, it seems that Word „Class" or full term „Social Class" belong to obscene words or it is completely insignificant to be reported or studied. After fall of communism (Berlin Wall Fall) it's very rare to see some serious article or analysis on „Class Issue". Does it mean that we have entered in „Classless society"? I guess not. But, in the era of divided world „Class Issue" dominated social sciences and real life in communist part of Globe. Almost everything that happens were explained by „Class antagonism" and „Class struggle". Karl Marx theory that History is „made on class struggle" were widely adopted as official theory and politics of governments in communist countries - China, Soviet Union, countries in Warsaw Pact and Yugoslavia.

Marx work „The Communist Manifesto" has become integral part of almost all programs and concepts of communist parties in countries that were ruled by communist party monopoly. According to Marx there were two classes – Proletariat and Bourgeoisie. Proletariat has no any means of production in possession, on other side, Bourgeoisie (Capitalists) posses all means of production. In order to live and survive workers, without means of production, are forced to sell their human labor to business owners. In 19th century and, probably, first half of last century this theory had worked pretty good. Today, in 21st century, since world is so diversified, this division to only two classes looks too simplified. According to Marx all owners of production means are privileged and rich, on the other side workers have nothing, except their human labor that sell at low rate. Workers, without any valuable assets in private property are, as a rule, poor, without any real chance to enter Bourgeoisie class. That was era of first industrialization, there were no division to „blue and white collars", rich owners were not, even, nor from a far, as rich as tycoons nowadays; there were no class of technical engineers and artists. Are all people who don't posses means of production poor, by definition. I guess not. Is Hollywood actor or pop rock mega singer, who has no any means of production, forced to sell his or her work for low wages. What about bestseller writers who earn extreme sums of money through royalties. They are rich people who sell their talent and artwork at very high price. Fault of Marxist theory is that it doesn't recognize rich people in class of workers, all workers are poor, and all capitalists rich. Think of businessmen whose companies have bankrupted and assets confiscated for debt settlement. Next, migration from working to bourgeoisie class was almost impossible, chances for worker's children and grandchildren to move to owners class were almost zero.

Although some new surveys show that increased number of classes in modern society (Great British Class Survey finds seven social classes in UK), remains basic division to three class – upper, middle and lower classes. Economic capital remains basic and dominant factor of class designation, although some new indicators are included such as Cultural and Social Capital. It's usually linked that, mainly, people with more Economic Capital have more Cultural as well as Social Capital. Nobody can expect that people with low income have more ties, visit more concerts or spend holidays on exotic islands in 5 star hotels 5,000 miles far from home. Thinking different way in Price-tag world, where nothing, except breathing air, is for free; seems to be more mocking than serious survey. Frankly, there are some rather frequent exceptions, in particular, in transitional societies, where, there is so called class of "controversial businessmen", which small number members became rich overnight. It is bizarre but they prefer striptease club than theater or opera, although they own yachts, luxury apartments, cars and millions of dollars on different accounts worldwide. Their Cultural Capital is illogical low in comparison to Economic Capital. Social capital is unproportional too, but having in mind quote "Money makes the world go round", as well as that social ties are sold and bought on "open market", they reach satisfactory level in this segment.

Although, set of various factors could be taken in consideration, **ECONOMIC** is still dominant in 21st as it was in 19th century.

Karl Marx thought in binary system of having or not having, today class issue is most sophisticated and compound question, **Economic** capital, factor, indicator, impact, variable, call it however or whatever you want remains dominant, even, today. Some new indicators, such as, education, occupation, cultural and social capital are introduced, but stubbornly claiming that they are dominant and neglected comparing to Economic capital, is hypocrisy and mocking this sensitive issue.

On the other hand, can we transition countries "controversial businessmen", call class elite or, rather, primitive, having in mind their cultural, or social capital. Is a person who live slightly above average, go to theater, read books, donate some money to needy, regarding other than economic capital, elite or somewhere between lower and middle class. Unfortunately, I live in country there are pretty good number of examples for mentioned. Many of my high school friends after receiving diploma at Belgrade University have left for overseas countries (Australia, New Zealand, US and Canada). As engineers and computer programmers they belong to middle class in countries they live in. They have well paid jobs, nice houses, good cars, go at least twice a year on vacation outside country they reside. Although 40 years ago our standard of living was at approximately same level, today they live in upper class comparing to me, with income, at least, 10 times higher than mine. One can conclude that it's all about money and assets – that means economic capital. Serbia as part of former

Yugoslavia that was stable middle developed country 25 years ago, slided to last from stable middle developed country to last position in Europe due to unfavorable conditions and extremely bad and unwise politicians. From member of lower middle class I slided to poor, my cultural and social capital is devastated by bed financial status. Once I have been frequent theater and concer goer, book reader, fan of trips abroad, nowadays almost all income is spent on basic needs (board and lodging). My pockets are empty for creating and keeping social ties, spending on cultural events and goods, having nice hobbies.

Economy is prerequisite of all other infrastructure, that means, Economic capital is primary and dominant in social class defining, not cultural, or social capital. Rich people can have spare time for parties, many friends, can fly to distant exotic destinations, poor not. Let's remind you to Erich From masterpiece „To have or to be"; that dilemma doesn't exist in this price-tag world where making piles of money become not just tool but final goal of new generations worldwide. No choice between „To have" and „To be"; If one has, he is. On the other hand, If one has not, there is no any chance, for him or her „To be", as simple as that, it's not affordable to him (her). He can afford only bare survival, in some case, even that is impossible.

Therefore, taking economic indicator for class definition still works, although, new stratification according to some other elements is significant and valid too, but, just, under condition, that economy is not pushed into the background.

World blondes, for instance, cannot be class. What is common to Finnish, Russian and American blonde, except hair color. Criteria must be carefully selected, otherwise risk of wrong conclusions are inevitable. Namely, according to media and political establishment and public, it seems that we live in classless world (existinf of one class is classless society too, there must be, at least, two).

Insisting, or even mentioning „class issue" could make problems; nobody needs conflicts, protests and strikes, so it's better get rid of that term, no matter what reality looks like.

State want us to pay taxes, CEOs and managers to work well and be loyal to corporation, no matter what we think and how we live. According to criterion of employment all employed in same corporation have same goal and behavior code. Why not call them „Coca Cola or McDonald's Class", no matter some work for $15,000 per year, while income, including binuses, of top CEOs in same company could reach $10,000,000 for same period. Entry level workers as well as CEOs are deployed to make company profit higher, keep good market position, no matter how much is compensation for their work.

What is common to entry level worker with miserable income and CEO?!? Probably, feeling that all are members of one team playing the hard game on cruel and umpredictable market. Both of them work for better of company, for higher profits. Simple job workers are under higher pressure,since they are, in the case of getting worse, fired first. It's very rare that CEOs are fired, and if it happen they get bonuses higher than lifetime income of ordinary workers.

That's why term „Class", or „Social Class" is not IN. It's anachronism, out of date unnecessary word. Fighting for bare life survival, or our private company survival on market, doesn't matter, make us belong to one class, no matter whether we spend our income for potatoes and bread, or travel around the Globe in private plane or luxury yacht.

However, enthusiasts can study class differentiation and stratification using criteria as if they deal with motor vehicles or motor boats (how many horse powers or kilowats is car or truck engine, or how long is boat, less or over 12 meters). It's not forbidden, although recommended by establishment, question is how much such results are worth for scientific study.

Simple calculation that tells almost nothing could be.

Poorest, people who are on welfare, those earning between $12,000 and $30,000, over $30,000 to $50,000, between 50,000 and $100,000. Next between $100,000 and $500,000, then between $500,000 and million dollars, and the richest class over $1,000,000.

Using simple figures, without any decent explanation of reasons and structure, (as shown above) is more like phone guide than analysis. Finally, maybe we have already entered to classless society, as Marx quoted that „Communism would be classless society". That means „no classes, no class issue surveys and analyses".

What we really need

I would start this chapter with short biographical story that is good example for some ideas that will come later. I remember when I bought first color CRT TV, made in Nis, town located on Serbian south, in 1984. It has even worked in year 2006, when replaced with newer, more modern model – Samsung produced in South Korea. Number of factories that produced consumers electronics in my country Yugoslavia, 1984 was **four**, in 2006. My country was just part of former Yugoslavia, now called Serbia with **zero** number of consumer electronics. This, factory counting is just small digression from main topic – our **real** needs. However, some in globalization shaping the world got wings to fly, some lose or, better say crippled, so only moves were creeping.

New TV had better design, higher image resolution and stereo sound, and remote controller, of course. Even new CRT TV works pretty good. Each single second we have almost 100 TV channels at click of remote button. Do we need so many channels to enjoy, after 10 hours of bullshit (8 hours at work and 2 hours in city traffic)? Not, sure. Most of us will spend spare time frequently clicking remote controller, paying attention to each channel several minutes, then flat out and totally brainwashed next action would be jumping to bed and quick sleep for another business day. Let's go back to our TV.

Today, TV sets are very thin with perfect image and sound, but its lifetime is at best 5 years. Seller in one Belgrade downtown luxury consumers electronics salloon has said to me „No matter how much you pay, no matter whether you buy branded or unknown model, all TVs are produced to last 5 years. If, in some case its lifetime be longer you are lucky guy"

Next problem is that there is nothing to fix and repair on new TVs, they are without parts, just one solid item, thin panel. If something get wrong the only option is to throw it to litter. Regarding old fashioned TV, made in Yugoslavia that I used almost 23 years, I have changed resistor twice, worth not more than $10.

However, technology has its own rules we can take it or pretending not to see what`s going on.Latter, of course, does not mean that we are nof affected by hi-tech gadgets. The issue is whether humans need such speed and way of introduction of new technology. It seems that we serve tecnology not technology us, ultrafast pace of consumers technology development has become „raison d` etre" per se (reason of existence). Not all gadgets are equally useful, for instance I see mobile phones as „disturbing devices", comparing to broadband high speed internet, that I consider one of the greatest inventions in human history. How many times I have wished to destroy my mobile when ringing during drive through roundabout trafic, or getting of the city bus. I know that in case of emergency hospital won't send helicopter ambulance if I get sick, in the meantime I usually get tons of calls and sms messages from absentminded bosses, and wife who want use mobile as 24 hours checking device. Maybe, global referendum on consumers technology gadgets is desperately needed to see what people think.

Just imagine how wonderful world would have been if money had been invested in medical and natural sciences instead in computer, robot and telecommunications technology. Cancer and aids would be cured as simple as ordinary flue, average life of ordinary Earth citizen would be 100 years, or even more... Even some other than computer based technology, subgroups (as traffic means, for instance) were hardly neglected. Flight between Paris and New York lasts exactly as half a century ago, most cars still use petrol as fuel. If scientist had been busy with mentioned type of researches, Paris-New York flight would have lasted one hour and cars would have been battery or solar energy operated.

Fundamental Redistribution of Reasearch & Development costs is needed due to more even development of ALL Science & Technology not just computer based and telecommunications. In budgeting, Politicians, CEOs and other VIPs must take in consideration benefits of all, ordinary people not just profit rates of corporate establishments.

Next issue is matter of gradualism. Urgent or immediate „Fast as Lightning" action is something that is hard shock and stress to organism of almost all human beings. Most prefer ease of paragliding, ordinary sliding speed – Gradual, phase to phase approach to huge, significant changes in their lives. It is in full accordance to Human nature. People organism is not, at this point, structured as computer chip, to execute billion operations in one millisecond, neither it will be soon. However, we see constant breaching of this „Gradualism principle" each day. Let's take as an example, graduated students who have just started to work. They should work shorter, not 8 hour shifts, first 2 to 3 years to adapt themselves to quite new corporate lifestyle. Otherwise, their organism (body & mind) is shocked after 4 to 5 years enjoying freedom of University student lifestyle. Same applies to the people approaching retirement age. Viceversa, their assignment is to adapt themselves from „corporate life" full of routine boring duties to „total freedom" of retired persons. Why hot gradual reducing of working hours from regular 8 to 4 hours, in last decade, or 5 years before retirement. Corporate Human Resources Departments should pay attention to this important issue if they want to meet demands of mentioned groups of people. Unfortunately, reality is different - People after 40 years of 8 hour work, 5 days of week, leave office in the period of snapping fingers. Nobody thinks how bad is for health (mental, in particular) of these people who are old at the time of retirement. Corporations, probably, won't benefit from that, but gradual increasing or decreasing working hours (depenting which group we refer to) would be much better for them. Instead of gradual approach humans must cope with permanent and almost immediate changes in everyday life. As Alvin Toffler predicted in his book

FUTURE SHOCK 40 years ago, everything that surround us in the near future would be more and more temporary; most people sticked to traditional way of life, when significant changes had taken, at least, one generation, would slide to state of mental shock. Artificial hyperproduction of various merchandise and artificial creating of new human needs, on daily basis, is justified by original human will. Is that really so?

Maybe most people would renounce 90 percent of their dreams of being wealthy just to have 15 to 20 percent higher income;or get rid of all, or almost all, hi-tech gadgets for the sake of job security. **Steady** job that brings **decent** income is something that we desperately need. Who will answer question WHY SOMEBODY PREVENT US FROM FULFILLING THAT GOAL?

Recent surveys by selected countries show that **people are more afraid of job loss than of death.** It sounds, at the same time, sad, horrible and ridiculous. Such result should and must attract URGENT attention and, of course, appropriate measures aiming to change this. Politicians, businessmen, economists, sociologists and psychiatrists must pay serious and urgent attention to this issue. Unfortunately, there were no, almost any, serious reaction from the people, who are in charge of solving such issues, people who are creators and trendsetters of our business and life enviroment. Human Being is living natural creature, not Corporate sophisticated product. Next, just imagine what people are ready to do to get or keep their job in such case.

That is Moral issue. Instead, VIPs deliver empty speeches with empty phrases and slogans on democracy, freedom, market rules, debt crisis, necessity of killing public and state sector in economy, privatization of all resources (schools, hospitals, police, and even graves). Ordinary people are supposed (or better say set) to believe when looking them at TV, internet or in printed media. The rules of mechanics that applied to robots, computers and other new sophisticated machines are automitacally applied to Human Beings. Plug and Play humans, day by day, become reality. To participate in „Game" called „Living life" one is supposed, just to be switched on, by plugging. Unfotunately, unplugging, is much more difficult, if not impossible. In the world of extreme hyperproduction of various merchandise and services, there are no DIFFERENT CONCEPTS (SYSTEMS). High speed changes, uncertainty, overchoicing, temporary value systems is something we CANNOT be unplugged from.

People are not allowed to be willingly UNPLUGGED from offered one System; if they try they cope with survival issue. Mainstream media, politician, experts and other VIPs present such SYSTEM (Concept, Ideology, Religion) as something we cannot live without. According to them it is unavoidable as aging or death. There is no any chance to escape from that „Imposed System", without very serous consequences. Just look at example of homosexual people, who were treated in era of our fathers and grandfathers as sick people, exercising that lifestyle on public places was considered criminal offence for which imprisonment was threatened.

Nowadays, they have almost all rights that have opposite sex couples (adopting and bringing up children, etc...). Are our brains set to accept such changes, according to Plug & Play rule?

To address this sensistive issue I would quote small excerpt from Toffler's book FUTURE SHOCK

"Thus when we hurl a man into outer space, we surround him with an exquisitely designed microenvironment that maintains all these factors within livable limits. How strange, therefore, that when we hurl a man into the future, we take few pains to protect him from the shock of change. It is as though NASA had shot Armstrong and Aldrin naked into the cosmos.

It is the thesis of this book that there are discoverable limits to the amount of change that the human organism can absorb, and that by endlessly accelerating change without first determining these limits, we may submit masses of men to demands they simply cannot tolerate.

We run the high risk of throwing them into that peculiar state that I have called future shock. We may define future shock as the distress, both physical and psychological, that arises from an overload of the human organism's physical adaptive systems and its decision-making processes. Put more simply, future shock is the human response to overstimulation. Different people react to future shock in different ways. Its symptoms also vary according to the stage and intensity of the disease. These symptoms range all the way from anxiety, hostility to helpful authority, and seemingly senseless violence, to physical illness, depression and apathy.

Its victims often manifest erratic swings in interest and life style, followed by an effort to "crawl into their shells" through social, intellectual and emotional withdrawal. They feel continually "bugged" or harassed and want desperately to reduce the number of decisions they must make". (Alvin Toffler, Future Shock).

I will finish this chapter with one of my aphorisms that I considered as a solid basis for some new surveys - We live virtually but die for real.

Summary

This is, probably, the hardest job to pull out, or create, 5 to 7 wisdom sentences that sound more like Proverb or God Commandment than recommendations (proposals) what to do to make this only world better place to live on. Most of Summary are zipped (compressed) version of topics described in previous chapter, although there are some new ideas.

WAR AS A WAY OUT – By analogy after two successive industrial revolutions, comes two world wars in rather short period of less than three decades. We are in the heart of The Third Industrial Revolution in which human beings are replaced by computers and robots. At this point nobody can describe how The Fourth Industrial Revolution will look like. Of course, it doesn't mean that it will be followed by The Third World War. However, War cannot be way out, even if it leads to better more humane and just world. Next World War will be ten or dozen times more devastating, than first two world wars taking together. Nowadays there is a set (not one), of countries with nuclear, biological and/or chemical warfare. Number of living people would be outcome by dead or wounded. However, even if that terrible fact was put aside, outcome of, potential, Global war still would remain fully unpredictable. Namely, according to the current balance of power, World after next Global War, would likely be more unjust and much worse place to live for majority, with high probability, that differences between rich and poor would be school example of Ancient Rome or Greek slavery system. So, let's forget even thinking of war, in particular, world one as any tool for settlement of hot global issues.

CUTS AND AUSTERITY MEASURES AS BOGEYMAN FOR ADULTS

If *everyone owes everyone* and no one can pay his or her debt something MUST BE wrong with debt standards. That means that debt standards and ratio must be revised. If teacher give all students bed marks, who should be criticized, teacher or students? If there is, almost no woman, without prior sexual experience at age 25, should we choose virgin ladies for marriage, or, maybe, put aside that fact as irrelevant.

Modern politicians, economists and influential VIPs are in labyrinth of XIX century dogma; they rush as bulls into red, trying to solve XXI century issues by sticking to XIX century dogmas. That, certainly, will not ever work. We are frightened and brainwashed, on daily basis, by worldwide cuts and austerity measures feeling like criminals who stolen and spent that money. Who is guilty – all of us or somebody who really made debts. Without individual specification of those in charge of "

It seems more that primary goal is to „Keep tensions in crowds" than getting global economy for better.

Bogeyman is imaginative being used by adults to frighten children into compliant behavior.

However, maybe keeping „State of Fear for Masses" is efficient tool to keep „Privileges of a Very Few";and that is psychology not economics issue.

COSTS TAG VS. HUMAN BEINGS WELFARE WORLD

This is very controversial topic, difficult even to discuss, not ot mention some fundamental changes towards more humane world. People well-being should be put in front of profit margins of companies and rich individuals. Happy, healthy, or at least, satisfied Majority of people must be Primary Goal not earnings. More jobs, less crimes and sickness, Decent standard of living of most people, not extreme luxury of a very few ultrarich VIPs must be something we all fight for. It`s really horrible and unbelievable that in 21st century people die from hunger (BBC News Headline - Somalia famine 'killed 260,000 people'. Nearly 260,000 people died during the famine that hit Somalia from 2010 to 2012, a study shows. Half of them were children under the age of five, says the report by the UN and the US-funded Famine Early Warning Systems Network (Fews Net).) Nor a single child should be allowed to starve to death, even in Africa. Such tragic events put enormous burden of shame on all of us, in particular, powerful people who can act to prevent such things. As Human Beings we must act in humane way. It`s our mission, isn`t it.

SCIENCE & TECHNOLOGY ISSUE – More proportional development of all sciences. It's obvious that research &

development efforts and funds in fields of computer based technology, telecommunications and robotics significantly outbalance those in natural sciences, medicine etc... Again, Science & Technology should not be in service of Corporations gains, but in service of well being of all people. That's true, modern computers are more compact, much smaller, more than 1,000 times faster with 10,000 (or so) larger data storage capacity than those used half a century ago, but flight between London and New York takes almost the same time, measuring in minutes.

GRADUALISM ISSUE – Gradual approach not „Fast as Lightning" speed in all deep revolutionary changes in society. That would be prevent human organism and mind from shock and mental instability keeping it in balance. Good example for mentioned is Gradual reducing of working hours for people approaching retirement age.

STICKING TO BASIC NEEDS – If World is Global, linked and interconnected village, and if we, all live on and share this only planet Earth, Basic needs should be defined at Global level. That would be, let's say, kind of „Minimum wage" for all, employed and unemployed, black and white, Americans, Africans, Europeans or Asians. Social assistance funds - minimum funds per capita for living must be regulated by law worldwide. Although this measure sounds very bureaucratic (against free market and democracy principles) human beings (as term speaks per se) should act in humane way too.

Otherwise, CEOs and VIPs will keep changing their yachts more easily and more frequently than their employees and other people socks and underpants.

VIRTUAL VS. REAL WORLD – We live virtually, but die for real, is one of my numerous aphorisms. Namely, one gets an impression that real world is substituted by virtual. This applies to average and poor people, in particular. There is flood of hi-tech gadgets laptops, tablets, androids that make us feel we have been on holiday or concert without leaving apartment. Ultra high resolution, surround sound systems, 3D monitors are in mission of evoking reality of exotic island, or concert of some star singer.

There is no need to pay 2 to $3,000 for real trip to exotic island, or $200 for concert of famous singer, quite enough is to switch of personal computer and start „Enjoying substituted experience". That's, likely why computers and Hi-tech gadgets are getting cheaper day by day. Pretty good substitute for those who have not accomplish their dreams, dreams of wealth and happiness, they have toys in form of affordable hi-tech gadgets. However, as my aphorism at the beginning of this paragraph, says - still there is something in real world that cannot substituted by virtual.

ROLE OF POLITICIANS – When I look at modern politicians acting worldwide - presidents, prime ministers and ministers, leaders of big as well as leaders of small countries, I cannot not to remember NYPD slogan „To Serve & Protect". They use to behave as agents of rich and very rich, not ALL citizens. They think about ordinary people several weeks before election date; after winning elections, they usually act as if they got sudden amnesia. Politicians must be „buffer zone" and "middleman" between rich and poor, employers and employees, and other groups with opposed antagonistic interests. They are not or should not be, in any case, servants of wealthy tycoons. As they have very high degree of independence from ordinary people, they should keep same relation to wealthy VIPs too.

FAIR DISTRIBUTION OF INCOME AND WEALTH – It is likely one of most sensitive among hot issues nowadays. At the very beginning of global economic crisis in autumn 2008, BBC conducted online survey – More than 70 percent of people were for significant reducing of salary gap between workers and CEOs. Of course, nothing has happened, due to the unfortunate fact that telecommunications and internet is used, mainly, for spying and controlling crowds worldwide, not to making this world better place to live for ALL. This is not just economic, but psychological issue too – Why CEO per annum earnings in a company can exceed 10 or 20 million dollars, while simple low ranked workers work for less than $15,000. What is optimal gap for well being of ALL. It sounds ridiculous that top managers and CEOs have no incentives to work unless they earn at least $1,000,000 per month, employees in their company are supposed to be happy with $15,000 or slightly above.

State do not want to be involved in such issues, on the pretext, that it is not democratic, neither in good mood of free market economy. Government pays attention only to collecting taxes, not to fair distribution inside corporations, just proving its agent's and/or servaant's role of wealthy.

DEMOCRACY & FREEDOM VS. BUREAUCRACY & REGULATIONS

Multiparty system and voting freedom is something that is considered as symbol of democracy & freedom. On the other side too much regulations, state domination over economy is known as symbol of bureaucracy and low efficiency, that was usually linked to former communist countries. My question is – Can you teach starving people anything, not to mention democracy & freedom...Probably, not. Disappearing of strong and numerous members of middle class is something that state (government) should be blamed for. That is not, and never will be , for sure, corporations assignment. Closing eyes at rapid disappearing of middle class, increasing unemployment and poverty has nothing to do with democracy & freedom. Unfortunately, in some cases and periods, temporary sticking to more regulations and bureaucratic measures are necessary to protect freedom and democracy. People under age of 18 are not allowed to pubs, or in porno cinema. Maybe some teenagers of 17 are more mature than some people who are 20. It's bureaucratic rule. Why not put law limits 1:10, or 1:12, on earnings gaps; that could be good solution to protecting or, even, revival of middle class, for instance. Traffic Law, in modern democratic multiparty Serbia, where I live, has at least 10 new bureaucratic articles than 30 years ago when Serbia was part of Yugoslavia under Communist Dictatorship. Of course, explanation is that all is done for the safety of all participants in traffic, according to European rules.

Thanks

I would rather skip this chapter due to fact I cannot pull out nor a single person who made me write this short electronic book. Authors usually, use to list a group of people who contribute their works significantly. No matter whether „contributors" are children, parents, husband, aunt and/or uncle who pay for book preparation and some basic marketing; or, maybe, good colleagues who hide from chiefs and managers authors absence from job. Regarding my family, colleagues and/or friends this was, writing of E-book „Crossroads and/or Illusions" was, literally, top secret, covert operation. As simple as that, I didn't want to bother them with something that is not commercial project with high earnings.

Namely, I live in Serbia, civilization where, at this point, each move is precisely measured by money that brings. However, that which any concrete humans are not directly involved in my E-book project, does not mean that there were no impacts to me regarding some trends, events and happenings.

Some great revolutionary changes in telecommunications technology that resulted in fast broadband internet on one side and political events connected to bloody civil war break up of my country (Yugoslavia).

These two big factors (one technological and one political) have become my obsessions and fascinations, during last two decades, that, as simple as that „force & drive" me to write mentioned E-book. I feel as Alice in Wonderland seeing how telecommunications and internet change our lives in, mainly positive way. Unfortunately, there is dark, negative side that sparked idea of E-book creation – that is break up of my country to 6, some say 7 tiny countries started in 1991. It has nothing to do with nostalgia, but with fact that independent and sovereign Socialist Federative Republic of Yugoslavia had specific and unique system of so called Workers Self-management where factories and companies were owned by workers and employees not the state or capitalists.

Comparing that system to today's globalization is more like comparing different civilizations than systems. People who once lived in Yugoslavia, Poland, Russia know it well—basic social values, economic relations, interpersonal communication, lifestyles, individual freedoms of thinking and moving were completely different.

However, Yugoslavia, comparing to other communist countries, was „World per se". Safety of middle class lifestyle of most employed people was substituted by extreme insecurity of good steady jobs, low wages and miserable lives. This is, most likely, a view of the biggest loser in New World Order procedures called Serbia. Economic standard of living is more like alimentation than full income (average Serbs are at less than 1/3 of standard of Yugoslavian before break up).

Once at the top in group of mid developed European countries Serbia as the largest republic of former Yugoslavia is at steady last, or next to last position for almost two decades. This book is not written in conventional manner of an American or British writer, or expected, well known, apologetic style of former dissident from some Warsaw Pact country that was once occupied by Soviet Union. This „Rear Ground Zero View" of greatest loser, country where almost 60 per cent of people work for low wages struggling for survival.

Finally, reminding to Erich Fromm work *To Have or To Be* dilemma. My firm standpoint is - that writing books is in function of Human Being TO BE fulfillment goal, although in my country it's old fashioned way of thinking. TO HAVE is in trend – assets accumulations, luxury good and services as well as money inflow to accounts is even obsession of most University professors, not just ordinary and rich people. However, nor money, neither books can make somebody happy, but, I guess, that bottom line is - that writing has lot to do with nature and dignity of Human Being.

About the Author

Aleksandar Krzavac, the Author of e-book "Crossroads and/or illusions" published his first E-book in 2011 "Close Your Eyes the Future Has Just Begun"; e-book of, mainly, satirical aphorisms and cartoons that was supposed challenge people to think out of everyday convenient life.

Krzavac was born in 1959 in Belgrade, the former Yugoslavian capital, where he spent his teenage years and his thirties in what is referred to in the West as a Communist dictatorship. Holder of a University degree in economics, e-book author Aleksandar Krzavac does not object to wasting his time writing.

The Author has published his aphorisms and cartoons in highly regarded Belgrade newspapers and magazines and a selection of Krzavac's cartoons are published on the Aydin Dogan Vakfi website at http://sanalmuze.aydindoganvakfi.org.tr/Gallery/CaricatureList.aspx?&PID=5761. Aphorisms of Aleksandar Krzavac have appeared in the New York Times bestselling author James Geary's website at http://www.jamesgeary.com. He is also the author of the satirical play, "Crazed and Confused," which deals with the breakup of Yugoslavia.

Entering "Perfect society" will force many writers to change their careers, since perfection cannot be criticized. Judging by this reality, we still have many years ahead of us to achieve

PERFECTION. So, he has been assigned to write critical book "Crossroads and/or illusions" that challenges some of New World Order Holy Principles.

At present Aleksandar is employed with Serbian Broadcasting Company on the position of journalist. He is married, father of three daughters.

References

Alvin Toffler, Future Shock

Erich Fromm, To Have or To Be

Forbes Billionaires 2013: The Richest People In The World
The names, numbers and stories behind the 1,426 people who control the global economy

John Maynard Keynes, The End of Laissez-Faire: The Economic Consequences of the Peace

Karl Marx, Das Kapital - Capital: Critique of Political Economy

Karl Marx, Communist Manifesto

Edvard Kardelj, Self-management and the Political System

CIA factbook – National debt by Country

Public debt, International Monetary Fund, April 2012

Eurostat IMF and 2013 Budget Summary Tables

A third industrial revolution, Manufacturing and innovation, special report, The Economist, April 21, 2012

Jeremy Rifkin, The Third Industrial Revolution: How Lateral Power Is Transforming Energy, the Economy, and the World

Jeremy Rifkin, Leading the Way to the Third Industrial Revolution and a New Distributed Social Vision for the World in the 21st Century

A New Model of Social Class? Finding from BBC's Great British Class Survey Experiment, April 2, 2013

Various news, reports, surveys and politicians' speech experts, mainly, over hot economic issues, published at BBC website

www.ingramcontent.com/pod-product-compliance
Lightning Source LLC
Chambersburg PA
CBHW022115170526
45157CB00004B/1642